A CELEBRATION OF OUR SAINTS

by
KEVIN BYRNE

ACKNOWLEDGEMENTS

I wish to thank
MISS BERNADETTE BOWES for
her beautiful illustrations.

I also wish to acknowledge the kind help of
CANON MAURICE ABBOTT and MISS VIRGINIA BOWES,
and particularly of
MISS MONICA HART
without whose help this book would not have been published.

First published 1996 by Countyvise Limited, 1 & 3 Grove Road, Rock Ferry, Birkenhead, Wirral, Merseyside L42 3XS in conjunction with the author Canon Kevin Byrne.

Copyright © Canon Kevin Byrne.

ISBN 0 9077 68 90 3

iii

CONTENTS

FOREWORD
by
Canon John P. Marmion

It is a privilege to introduce Canon Byrne's work, *A Celebration of Our Saints*, a manuscript which has been awaiting publication for some years. This is history, and it is our history. How important is that? I suppose the first importance of history is that it is roots, and roots are an underground source of energy. Rabbi Heschel says, 'The human soul is born with a past'. The prophetic monk, Thomas Merton, thought we should be obsessed with history. He wrote;

> The Marxian idea that the key to everything is found in history is, curiously enough, the basic idea of the Bible. We, the Christians, have forgotten this. We have reduced our religious thought to the consideration of static essences and abstract moral values. We have lost the dynamic sense of God's revelation of himself in history.

The Scottish poet who died recently, George Mackay Brown, also had this sense of the importance of history. Henry Ford may have thought it was bunk, but George thought that 'We cannot live fully without the treasure our ancestors have left us. Without the story — in which everyone, living, unborn and dead, participates — men are no more than bits of paper blown on the wind.'

Here you will find God's plenty, some of the best of the history from our roots. Among the saints (Canon Byrne in his introduction gives the basis for his choice) you will make your own choice. I was fascinated by St Plegmund and the little church at Plemstall. But there are well known figures and favourites here; St Cuthbert was always very popular; Edward the Confessor has his fan club; those who have visited Lindisfarne may turn to St Aidan; if you want a traveller, try St Wilfrid. And St Hilda was abbess of a double monastery of both monks and nuns, which met in the abbey church. A truly remarkable lady.

Canon Byrne has always been concerned with the value of our roots. He has given us some of the history of two parishes in *Through a Gridiron Darkly* (St Laurence's, Birkenhead) and *Behold We Live, St Mary's Congleton 1821-1993*. In addition, his *Three on the Hook* gives a picture of the dockers of St Laurence's and, together with this study of the saints, he has also covered some of the martyrs in *Nine Martyrs of the Shrewsbury Diocese*. This is considerable and valuable labour. How should we benefit?

In the homes there is a strong case for turning off the TV and sharing these treasures among the family. And having got something of the picture, you might (as a family) imitate Frank Delaney and go on pilgrimage. Or have you not yet seen *A Walk in the Dark Ages?* The illustrations — there are enough to get you interested. The saints have a clearer vision than the rest of us, and some knowledge of them gives better direction to our lives. Their friendship is worth cultivating, and many will thank Canon Byrne for his help in doing just that, and for even suggesting a prayer for each of them.

INTRODUCTION

My choice of pre-reformation English and Irish saints, plus a few more, who are venerated in our diocese, is disputable but now irrevocable, until a second edition. When Bishop Brown came to our newly created diocese of Shrewsbury in 1851, it occupied the area of Cheshire and Shropshire, as they then were, with the addition of six counties in North Wales, which were detached in 1895. When he dedicated the diocese to Our Lady Help of Christians, with St Winefride as Secondary Patron, and added St Peter of Alcantara's name to the cathedral, he gave us our first three saints. The rest is history.

The Romans tramped up and down our diocese from Wroxeter to Chester, making sorties on either side. There were christians among them. They built a church at Chester. Alban was the first English martyr from those days. He is one on our list.

The Romans left in 408, under pressure from Picts and Scots. Darkness descended on the land, with attacks from Angles, Saxons and Jutes. St Patrick was an early light on the horizon, but he shed it on Ireland, where he went in 432. Still, he does have a well in Bebington.

Pope Gregory took the initiative in our country, when he sent Augustine to Kent in 597. That was the year Columba died, who had already made his base on Iona, from which Aidan came to evangelise Northumbria and to make a nearer headquarters on Lindisfarne. These sixth and seventh centuries were rich in saints. Nearly all our present diocese was looked after by Chad at Lichfield. When Chester diocese was carved from it in 1541, Werburgh kept an eye on it from her shrine in that city. Oswald got himself killed in Oswestry, in defence of his realm, although one wonders why he travelled so deep into Mercia to do it. Milburga was the great apostle of Shropshire, from her monastery at Wenlock. Alcmund was buried at Lilleshall. Bede, who unlike Milburga rarely left his monastery, wrote all about everybody.

In the ninth century, Plegmund was the one who got away — from his hermitage near Chester—and finished up Archbishop of Canterbury. King Edward ruled us all, before the Normans came. The Danes had already arrived, but did not provide us with any saints. In the thirteenth century, St Thomas of Hereford surely visited the south end of our diocese, which was in his care.

Other saints on our list had churches dedicated to them because of their splendid selves, but their influence on the diocese has been casual rather than causal; we do not now know why their names were chosen.

As recorded in THE NINE MARTYRS OF THE SHREWSBURY DIOCESE, we had a wonderful crop of martyrs in the sixteenth and seventeenth centuries. That was our second phase.

It would be pleasant to envisage a post-reformation group of native saints and martyrs venerated in our diocese, but there are none to record. Teresa Higginson of Neston is an official non-starter. Edel Quinn, who went to Upton Hall Convent on the Wirral and is now buried in Nairobi near my brother, has recently been declared Venerable. Perhaps some young readers of these lives may be inspired by them, so to live as to qualify.

OUR LADY HELP OF CHRISTIANS
Principal Patron of the Diocese
Feast, May 24th

Gold crown surmounting oval shield.
Gold cross, silver monograms on a blue field.

The title originated in the sixteenth century, when it is found in the Litany of Loreto, which was approved by Clement VIII in 1601. Possibly the victors of Lepanto, visiting the shrine of Loreto, gave her that title.

The feast was instituted by Pope Pius VII for the Papal States, when he finally escaped Napoleon's clutches (six years of captivity) on May 24th 1815, the first anniversary of his return. This is now the patronal feast of Australasia; and the devotion was spread by St John Bosco and his Salesians.

Bishop Brown, the first bishop of our diocese, wrote on 11th September 1851 "The first meeting of the clergy of the new Diocese of Shrewsbury was held in Birkenhead. At the meeting it was unanimously agreed to petition the Holy See to place the diocese under the special patronage of Our Blessed Lady and to permit us to

1

call her our patroness under the title "HELP OF CHRISTIANS". All the bishops at that time of the restoration of the hierarchy made a similar decision, to put their dioceses under one or other of the titles of Our Lady.

Bishop Murphy, who quoted this letter in 1951, commenting on the progress of the church in the preceding century, adds "Our Lady Help of Christians has had her Lepanto even in this small portion of Christendom".

PRAYER AS IN THE BREVIARY
Lord, place deep in our hearts the love of Mary, our help. May we fight vigorously for the faith on earth and praise your victories in heaven. We make this prayer through Christ our Lord. Amen.

OUR LADY OF PITY
(Our Lady of Sorrows)
Feast, September 15th

When Bishop Murphy preached at the opening of the church of Our Lady of Pity in Harlescott, Shrewsbury, he referred to the statue of Our Lady in the nearby Battlefield church. "They carved in wood an image of the Mother of God and they placed the dead Christ on her knees: and they called her the Mother of Pity, Mother of Compassion, in the literal sense of the word, of one who has suffered with another".

Mater Dolorosa.
The emblem is a reference to the words of Simeon, "A sword will pierce your own soul ..." A red heart with gold wings and pierced by a silver sword with gold hilt, on a field of blue.

Our Lady of Pity was a late medieval title, recalling the thirteenth Station of the Cross; the taking down of the Body of Christ from the cross. Michaelangelo's Pieta is its most famous representation.

Shrewsbury *was* a battlefield in 1403, when Hotspur and his many Cheshire men were defeated by Henry IV with great slaughter on both sides; and they represented our Lady, in that chantry church, as mourning for them as she did for her Son.

The church at Greasby has the same title.

PRAYER AS IN THE MISSAL
Father, as your Son was raised on the cross, his mother Mary stood by him, sharing his sufferings. May your Church be united with Christ in his sufferings and death and so come to share in his rising to new life, where he lives and reigns with you and the Holy Spirit for ever and ever. Amen.

ST WERBURGH, VIRGIN (d.699)
Feast, February 3rd

Daughter of Wulfhere, king of Mercia, whose father was the fierce Penda, she was born in Staffordshire in the early seventh century. Her mother was Ermenilda, daughter of Erconbert, king of Kent. So she was of royal Saxon blood. Little is known of her life.

Rebuffing various suitors, she entered the abbey of Ely. So did her mother, when Wulphere died, and Werburgh probably succeeded her as abbess. She was then asked to reform the Mercian monasteries and founded new ones at Threckingham, Hanbury and Weedon. Tales of her gifts of prophecy and discernment are legion; and there is the story of the wild geese, wreaking havoc in the cornfields, which flew away immediately and for good at her command.

She died at

Daughter of the king of Mercia, St Werburgh took her vows at Chester. Her attribute is a goose because she is said to have commanded a flock of wild geese to cease destroying the standing corn in the fields around the Abbey. With down-bent necks they came to be shut into a barn until they repented.

3

Threckingham and was buried at Hanbury. Her body was still incorrupt nine years later. In 875 it was removed to Chester through fear of the Danes. The church of SS Peter and Paul there, on the site of the present cathedral, was re-dedicated to St Werburgh and St Oswald. Hugh Lupus made it a great Benedictine abbey. In the reign of Henry VIII, the abbey, later a cathedral, was sacked, and St Werburgh's relics, centre of pilgrimage, were scattered. The empty shrine has since been partly restored.

PRAYER
Father, your Son Jesus taught us to pray always. Your holy abbess Werburgh gave her life to prayer. May prayer lead us to your heavenly kingdom. We ask this through Christ our Lord. Amen.

Relevance to our Diocese
St Werburgh's church and school, Chester, continue that city's devotion to the Saint. St Werburgh's, Birkenhead, was so named because of the nearby ancient Priory's connection with Chester.

ST WALBURGA, VIRGIN (d. 779)
Feast, February 25th

When Richard, a West Saxon royal, went on pilgrimage to the Holy Land with his sons St Willibald and St Winibald, he entrusted his eleven year old daughter to Tetta, abbess of Winborne. This was a monastery famous for holiness and austerity, as well as learning. In her twenty six years there, Walburga was trained so thoroughly that she was later able to write the life of Winibald and an account in Latin of Willibald's travels. She is reckoned to be the first woman author of both England and Germany.

Her mother Winna was sister to St Boniface. When he was preaching the gospel successfully in Germany, his two nephews joined him. Then Tetta sent Walburga and many other nuns to take part, at the request of Boniface who was the first to call women to this apostolate. When a violent storm threatened their ship, Walburga prayed on deck and produced a miraculous calm. For two years she

4

stayed at Bischofsheim. In 761, by then skilled in medicine, she ruled a double monastery at Heidenheim, in succession to Winibald. There she remained until her death in 779.

Ozanam writes "Silence and humility have veiled the labours of the nuns from the eyes of the world; but history has assigned them their place at the very beginning of German civilisation. Providence has placed women at every cradleside".

Her relics were translated to Eichstadt in 870, on May 1st. The fact that this date coincides with a pagan feast for the beginning of summer and the revels of witches (Walpurgisnacht) is unfortunate. They are not connected. From the rock round her tomb medicinal oil still flows, used in miraculous cures.

St Walburga has an acquired role as protector of crops and therefore has three ears of corn among her attributes. This is possibly due to the confusion of her name with that of Waldborg, the pagan fertility goddess. She is also represented by an abbess's crozier, a flask of Walpurgis oil —and a crown and sceptre, possibly because she was a royal princess.

PRAYER
Father, Walburga left her home to pray and work in mission lands. Bless all those women who travel abroad to spread the good news of Christ. We ask this through the same Christ our Lord. Amen.

Relevance to our Diocese
St Walburga's church in Plowden was built by William Plowden. In a family so long rooted in the catholic faith, no doubt he had good reason to commemorate this Saxon abbess.

CATHOLIC ENCYCLOPEDIA (1912 edition)
At present the most famous of the oils of saints is THE OIL OF ST WALBURGA (Walburgis Oleum). It flows from the stone slab and surrounding metal plate on which rest the relics of St Walburga

in her church in Eichstadt in Bavaria. The fluid is caught in a silver cup, placed beneath the slab for that purpose, and is distributed among the faithful in small phials by the Sisters of St Benedict, to whom the church belongs.

A chemical analysis has shown that the fluid contains nothing but the ingredients of water. Though the origin of the fluid is probably due to natural causes, the fact that it came into contact with the relics of the saint justifies the practice of using it as a remedy against diseases of the body and the soul. Mention of the oil of St Walburga is made as early as the ninth century by her biographer Wolfhard of Herrieden.

ST CHAD, BISHOP   (d. 672)
Feast, March 2nd

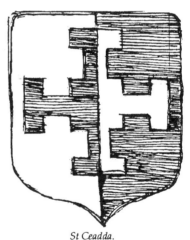

St Ceadda.
The colours of his symbol are red and silver

Possibly a Northumbrian, he was schooled at Lindisfarne, under Aidan, who sent him to Belmont, Ireland, for further education. Returning to help his brother St Cedd to establish a monastery at Lastingham, Yorkshire, he succeeded him as abbot. St Wilfrid went abroad to be consecrated bishop. He was destined for York, but he was away for so long that King Oswiu nominated Chad instead, who was consecrated by Wini of Sussex and two British bishops in 666. "He visited his diocese on foot, preaching the gospel; and seeking out the poorest and most abandoned persons to instruct and comfort in the meanest cottages and in the fields" (Bede).

Theodore judged his episcopal ordination to be doubtful, and rectified it, but gave the see of York to Wilfrid. Chad replied that he would willingly resign; that he had never thought himself worthy of such a responsibility; and that he had accepted only under obedience. Theodore was so impressed that he recalled him from Lastingham to be bishop of the Mercians. (He also insisted that Chad should ride a horse, in view of his great age and the size of his diocese).

Chad built a church at Lichfield and a monastery, where he lived with six or eight monks, when he was not visiting his flock. He also built a monastery at Barrow, Lincolnshire. After only three more years he died; and was buried at St Mary's. Then his body was transferred to the cathedral church of St Peter. In both these places there were miraculous cures. Thirty three ancient churches, including Chadkirk, Romiley, and several wells commemorate him. Some of his relics, saved from destruction by recusants, are at Birmingham catholic cathedral.

PRAYER
Father, help us to learn from the humility of St Chad, who confessed that he was unworthy of honour. May we too follow Jesus, who is meek and humble of heart. We ask this through Christ our Lord. Amen.

Relevance to our Diocese
All but the most southern part of our diocese, until Chester was created, was in St Chad's diocese of Lichfield; and his white cross appears in our diocesan coat of arms. Cheadle, the site of our St Chad's church, means Chad's hill. St Chad's Well (Shadwell) was on the east coast of Wirral, north of Job's Ferry.

ST PATRICK, BISHOP
APOSTLE OF IRELAND (c 390 - 461)
Feast , March 17th

The disputed birthplace of Patrick, a Romano-Briton is (not exactly pinpointed) in the West between the Severn and the Clyde. His father was the deacon Calpurnius. Patrick grew up an indifferent christian, but when he was carried off by Irish pirates, enslaved, and put to shepherding on the Slemish hills in Antrim, he turned to God in prayer and penance during six long years. He then escaped, managing to board a ship on the far coast, and returned home after weeks of semi-starvation. But he heard the Irish calling him in visions of the night, so he went to Gaul for training in the priesthood - perhaps to St Germanus of Auxerre. Probably the pope appointed him as bishop for Ireland, where he arrived in 432, in succession to St Palladius.

St Patrick's shield bears a red saltire on a silver field. He was known for the logical clarity of his preaching and used the three leaf shamrock to explain the Trinity. Snakes are his characteristic emblem as he is reputed to have expelled them and all poisonous animals from Ireland by the help of a staff which he claimed to have received as the gift of Christ.

He successfully confronted the High King and his druids at Armagh, where he set up his see. For the rest of his life he travelled round the country, consecrating many bishops and creating dioceses, ordaining priests, establishing monasteries. Kings of Dublin and Munster, the seven sons of the king of Connaught, were baptised by him, and he died at Down in Ulster. He was in constant danger of his life, but was Pauline in his acceptance of suffering for the souls of his people. He was not highly educated and was no intellectual, judging by his autobiography and his letter to Coroticus the slave-trader. Nevertheless, he was one of the great apostles in the history of the church; and Ireland has been the source of many other apostles, laity as well as priests.

PRAYER AS IN THE MISSAL

God our father, you sent St Patrick to preach your glory to the people of Ireland. By the help of his prayers, may all christians proclaim your love to all men. Grant this through our Lord Jesus Christ your Son, who lives and reigns with you and the Holy Spirit, one God, for ever and ever. Amen.

Relevance to our Diocese

With the huge Irish influx into our diocese up to the turn of the century, it is surprising that there is only one church dedicated to St Patrick - in Wellington, Telford. Birkenhead did have St Patrick's schools in 1858; and in Brotherton Park, Bebington, there is a St Patrick's well. (It is signposted, about a hundred yards from the entrance.) There is another in Burton, known locally as Hampston's Well.

By the law imposed by the Burton Manor Court, Patrick's Well had to be cleaned every year. All able bodied men of the village were required to help. If they failed to turn up they were fined sixpence. There were other wells and springs at Burton, but Patrick's Well was the most important. Originally the water was pumped into a barrel and delivered round the village by donkey cart at twopence a bucket. The presence of this well and the other at Brotherton Park, Bromborough, strengthens the belief, long held, that St Patrick traversed this area on his way to Ireland.

St Patrick's Well,
Brotherton Park,
Bromborough

9

EXTRACT FROM ST PATRICK'S BREASTPLATE
(as in the Breviary)

I bind unto myself today
The strong name of the Trinity:
By invocation of the same
The Three in One and One in Three.

I bind this day to me for ever,
By power of faith, Christ's incarnation,
His baptism in the Jordan River,
His death on the Cross for my salvation.
His bursting from the spiced tomb,
His riding up the heavenly way,
His coming at the day of doom,
I bind unto myself today!

I bind unto myself today
The power of God to hold and lead:
His eye to watch, his might to stay,
His ear to hearken to my need;
The wisdom of my God to teach,
His hand to guide, his shield to ward;
The Word of God to give me speech,
His heavenly host to be my guard!

Christ be with me, Christ within me,
Christ behind me, Christ before me,
Christ beside me, Christ to win me,
Christ to comfort and restore me,
Christ beneath me, Christ above me,
Christ in quiet, Christ in danger,
Christ in hearts of all that love me,
Christ in mouth of friend and stranger.

I bind unto myself the name,
The strong name of the Trinity:
By invocation of the same,
The Three in One and One in Three;
Of whom all nature hath creation,
Eternal Father, Spirit, Word:
Praise to the Lord of my salvation -
Salvation is of Christ the Lord.

10

ST ALCMUND, MARTYR (d.c. 800)
Feast, March 19th

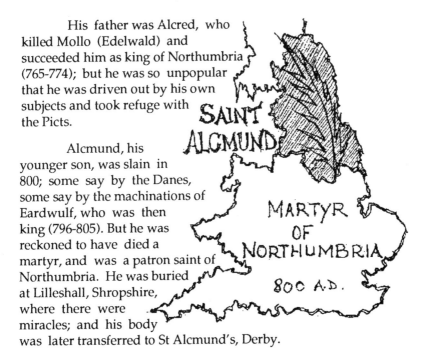

His father was Alcred, who killed Mollo (Edelwald) and succeeded him as king of Northumbria (765-774); but he was so unpopular that he was driven out by his own subjects and took refuge with the Picts.

Alcmund, his younger son, was slain in 800; some say by the Danes, some say by the machinations of Eardwulf, who was then king (796-805). But he was reckoned to have died a martyr, and was a patron saint of Northumbria. He was buried at Lilleshall, Shropshire, where there were miracles; and his body was later transferred to St Alcmund's, Derby.

PRAYER

Lord, we venerate the memory of your martyr, Alcmund. Hear his prayers for us, that we may also stand firm for your holy Name and for the kingship of our Lord Jesus Christ. Amen.

Relevance to our Diocese

Although we have no diocesan church in honour of St Alcmund, there are several ancient churches dedicated to him in Derbyshire and Shropshire, including the present St Alcmund's church in Shrewsbury. This was founded, they say, by Ethelfleda, daughter of King Alfred, who was also descended from the royal house of Northumbria.

ST STEPHEN HARDING, BISHOP (d.1134)
Feast, April 17th

St Stephen's shield bears a potent cross (a sign of power) in red, with a leopard's head inverted, on a white field.

Well born and well off, he was educated at Sherborne monastery, Dorset. With one companion, he set out for Scotland, Paris and Rome, reciting the psalter each day, otherwise proceeding in silence and meditation. He joined St Robert at the monastery of Molesme, but left because the monks were too lax. The Pope ordered him to return, but although he was the Superior, he could not get the monks to reform.

So in 1098 he went to Citeaux with Robert, Alberic and twenty one monks. There they built, with their own hands, a wooden monastery in a marshy wilderness, where they practised a severe regime. He was third abbot after the death of Alberic. He himself wrote a copy of the Latin Bible — no mean achievement. The Duke of Burgundy withdrew his patronage, because he was debarred from the cloister. Stephen had to beg from house to house. Sickness killed off the majority of the monks. No one else would join because the life was too strict for them. In answer to Stephen's prayers, St Bernard turned up with thirty followers, in 1112. The Order then flourished; and Stephen founded thirteen more monasteries in the next eight years.

Stephen is regarded as the principal founder of the Cistercian Order. He initiated annual visitations, assemblies of abbots: wrote the Carta Caritatis, a constitution copied by other orders; and the usages of Citeaux. He was asked to mediate between the king of France and the pope. He retired as abbot in 1133, after 25 years; and died the following year.

PRAYER

Father, you made Stephen Harding a founder of a great Religious Order. Help us to organise our own lives, so that we can follow faithfully the way of Christ. We ask this through Christ our Lord. Amen.

Relevance to our Diocese

A temporary chapel in Market Drayton was opened in 1883 named St Thomas Aquinas. Mr Egerton Harding provided a partial endowment. In 1886 he gave the land and erected both church and presbytery on it at his own expense. They commemorated St Thomas Aquinas AND St Stephen Harding. There were stained glass windows of both saints. Mass was said weekly for some years at the home of the Harding family. Mr Harding's gift was in thanksgiving for his conversion.

BUTLER'S LIVES

The Cistercian monks came over also into England in the time of St Stephen. (Their monasteries are still well known — Waverley, Tintern, Rievaulx and Fountains). The extreme austerity and sanctity of the professors of this order, which did not admit any relaxation in its discipline for 200 years, were a subject of astonishment and edification to the whole world ... (Many authors) mention with amazement their rigorous silence, their abstinence from flesh meat; and for the most part from fish, eggs, milk and cheese; their lying on straw, long watchings from midnight to morning, and austere fasts; their hard labour in cultivating desert lands to produce the pulse and herbs on which they subsisted; their piety, devotion and tears in singing the divine office; the cheerfulness of their countenances breathing a holy joy in pale and mortified faces; the lowliness of their buildings ...

ST GEORGE, MARTYR, PATRON OF ENGLAND
(3rd/4th Century)
Feast, April 23rd

All we can assert about St George is that he was regarded as one of the great martyrs of the Eastern church; and that he suffered, probably at Lydda in Palestine and probably in the time of Constantine. Pope Gelasius in 495 includes him among those saints "whose names are justly reverenced amongst men, but whose actions are only known to God". (This cuts out the legend of the dragon slaying, which emerged in the late Middle Ages).

He was certainly an historical figure. Pilgrims to the Holy Land in the 6th and 8th centuries testify to his cult and to churches dedicated to his name. St George's church at Doncaster was opened in 1061. The Crusaders brought home a devotion to him. The white ensign (red St George's cross on a white background) is of medieval origin and was flown on the king's ship round the time of Crecy (1334 - 1349). The Order of the Garter, of which St George is principal patron, was founded in 1347.

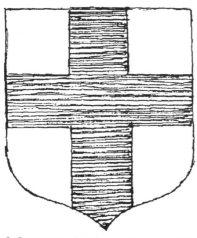

St George was a christian warrior whose shield became the badge of the English from the days of Richard Coeur-de-Lion. His arms are borne by the Order of the Garter. Colours: a red cross on a silver shield.

For some time St Edward the Confessor and St Edmund shared the honour of being English patron saints, but after Agincourt, in 1415, when Henry V spoke of St George as the patron saint, his feast became one of the most important in the land. 160 ancient churches are dedicated to him. He is the patron saint of many other places, including Portugal, Armenia, Ethiopia, Venice and Genoa. In Germany he was one of the fourteen auxiliary saints.

PRAYER AS IN THE MISSAL

Lord, hear the prayers of those who praise your mighty power. As St George was ready to follow Christ in suffering and death, so may he be ready to help us in our weakness. We ask this through our Lord Jesus Christ, your Son, who lives and reigns with you and the Holy Spirit, one God, for ever and ever. Amen.

Relevance to our Diocese

Our only church dedicated to St George is in Whitchurch.

ST MILBURGA, VIRGIN (664 - 728)
Feast, May 19th

By residential qualifications alone, Milburga is 'our most important diocesan saint'. She is thought to have been born near Bridgnorth in 664. Her father was Merewalh, sub-king of the Magonset (South Shropshire and Herefordshire) and her mother was Domneva, daughter of the christian king of Kent. Milburga was the cousin of St Werburgh; and she had two uncles, Ethelbert and Ethelred, as well as two sisters, Mildred and Mildgith, who were saints. When she was thirteen, she was sent to boarding school at Chelles, a Saxon monastery in Northern France, where she studied "languages, music, embroidery, calligraphy, scripture and liturgy".

She entered Wenlock abbey in 682, one of the magnificent seven double monasteries of England — like St Hilda's at Whitby — founded by her father with the assistance of St Botolf. When the first abbess Liobsynde retired, Milburga succeeded her and remained there for forty years. Her life was not shut in. She acquired about one third of Shropshire as abbey lands, as well as smaller areas around Brecon. Those villages and hamlets she visited and provided with churches and priests. Barrow, two miles from Wenlock, is one of the earliest of these.

She is credited with miracles even in her lifetime,

Some geese which were damaging the crops around the St Milburga's Abbey at Wenlock were driven away by her prayers, never to return. She had miraculous powers of healing which continued after her death.

and the geese in Corve valley obeyed her orders to stop away from her lands for many centuries. More remarkable still is the fact that the Danes, invading after her death, never entered her properties, due to

15

her intercession, it was said, and the Danelaw boundary merely borders them. The Normans acknowledged all the Shropshire properties in the Domesday book.

Milburga died in 728. The present church of the Holy Trinity was an enlargement of the nuns' chapel. The monks had their own, over which the basilica of St Milburga was erected. Her relics were discovered in the former church, by accident, in 1101; and were placed in a shrine at St Milburga's. Here there were many well established miracles, strictly investigated and confirmed by Bishop Odo of Ostia, sent for that purpose by the pope. Her relics were burned by the reformers in 1547.

PRAYER

Lord, we praise you for the prayerful life and the pastoral care of this diocesan saint. Hear her prayers on our behalf. We ask this through Christ our Lord. Amen.

Relevance to our Diocese

In view of the long life and unremitting pastoral care of St Milburga in Shropshire, one would expect Wenlock to be a place of pilgrimage for the whole diocese. Our church of St Milburga is in Church Stretton, but our church in Much Wenlock is called St Mary Magdalene. The chapel which preceded it from 1939 to 1955 had been called St Milburga's.

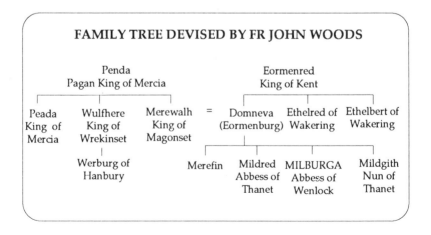

FAMILY TREE DEVISED BY FR JOHN WOODS

	Penda			Eormenred		
	Pagan King of Mercia			King of Kent		
Peada	Wulfhere	Merewalh	=	Domneva	Ethelred of	Ethelbert of
King of	King of	King of		(Eormenburg)	Wakering	Wakering
Mercia	Wrekinset	Magonset				
	Werburg of		Merefin	Mildred	MILBURGA	Mildgith
	Hanbury			Abbess of	Abbess of	Nun of
				Thanet	Wenlock	Thanet

ST BEDE, CONFESSOR, DOCTOR OF THE CHURCH (673 - 735)
Feast, May 25th

Born near Jarrow, he was only seven when he was entrusted to the monks of Wearmouth; but he was soon moved to Jarrow, where he became a monk, and in 703 a priest. He rarely moved out of that monastery for the rest of his life, and then only to Lindisfarne and York. "I have spent the whole of my life in that monastery, devoting all my pains to the study of the holy scriptures: and amid the observance of monastic discipline and the daily charge of singing in the church, it has ever been my delight to learn or teach or write. "

"To see him pray, one would have thought he left himself no time to study; and when we look at his books, we admire he could have found time to do anything else but write".

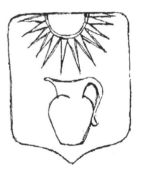

By his ECCLESIASTICAL HISTORY OF ENGLAND (713), he was the father of English history. He left a martyrology of 114 saints, 25 scripture commentaries. "All the sciences and every branch of literature were handled by him" *(Butler)*; natural history, principles of Aristotle, astronomy, arithmetic, the calendar, grammar, music, hymnody and verse. He was proficient in both Latin and Greek. In 1899, Leo XIII nominated him Doctor of the church.

Referred to as the 'Venerable Bede', his emblem indicates his great faith. A gold pitcher with the light from heaven — silver rays emanating from the gold centre on a blue field.

He worked on his translation of St John's Gospel into Old English up to the last moment. Then, when all the monks were gathered round him - "It is now time for me to return to him who made me; and gave me a being when I was nothing … The time of my dissolution draws near. I desire to be dissolved and to be with Christ. Yes, my soul desires to see Christ, my King, in his beauty".

PRAYER AS IN THE MISSAL

God our Father, you gave St Bede his learning for the glory of your Church. May we benefit by his wisdom and share his love of prayer. We ask this through Christ your Son, our Lord. Amen

Relevance to our Diocese

St Bede's, Weaverham, was cut off from St Wilfrid's, Northwich in 1950. Perhaps the one Saxon saint's name suggested the other. For some years there was a St Bede's school in Wallasey.

AUGUST MOLINIERE
(quoted in Mourret Thompson's
HISTORY OF THE CATHOLIC CHURCH)

Bede wrote an excellent survey of the national traditions of England, and in this work the form is of equal merit with the contents. Bede's example is there to prove what a small group of active, enlightened people can do for civilisation. Converted less than a century before by a handful of Italian missionaries, Great Britain became an intense home of learning and faith and soon paid back to the continent the services it received from Italy. (Northumbria was certainly not converted by Italian monks, but it is true that all Saxon England turned its eyes to Rome).

LAVISSE

All eyes were turned towards the capital of the world. Each year large numbers of Anglo-Saxon pilgrims set out; monks and nuns, priests, bishops and nobles. When they came in view of the holy city, they stopped to contemplate the sight and knelt in prayer. Their first visit was to the tomb of St Peter ... A century sufficed for Britain, conquered by priests, to become a papal province, as a century had sufficed for Gaul, conquered by the legions, to become one the most Roman of the imperial provinces.

ST AUGUSTINE OF CANTERBURY, BISHOP OF THE ENGLISH (d.c. 605)
Feast, May 27th

Pope Gregory had long desired to evangelise the English; and in 597 he sent Augustine, prior of St Gregory's monastery on the Caelian Hill, with thirty monks and their interpreters, to Ethelbert, king of Kent. This was after a long journey, during which they had become fearful and wished to turn back, but the pope encouraged them. Ethelbert's wife Bertha was a christian, who used the old Roman church of St Martin for her worship. Augustine landed on the Isle of Thanet, and after a cautious welcome, the king listened to his preaching and was eventually baptised. Although the king left his people perfectly free to choose, 10,000 were baptised on Christmas day 597.

Augustine established a monastery at Canterbury, Ss Peter and Paul; and after he was consecrated bishop at Arles, built his cathedral there too. He did not range widely over the south of England, but was to make a bishop in London and one in Rochester.

He requested the pope for more manpower. From these new recruits came Mellitus (London, for the East Saxons), Justus (Rochester), Paulinus (York). In sending him the pallium, the pope empowered him to appoint twelve bishops in the south; and the bishop of York to appoint another twelve. This did not fully develop, but it foreshadowed the future.

Augustine met British bishops, and asked them to combine with him in evangelising the Saxons (and to observe the Roman Easter). The Britons refused, partly because of their anti-Saxon feelings, and partly because they resented Augustine's claim to precedence. Ten years later the

The cross and pallium indicate St Augustine's archiepiscopal rank. The lily is believed to be included because he died in May, Mary's month.

Saxons killed large numbers of them, as Augustine had predicted.

He consulted the pope and received his advice in letters still extant, which relate to liturgy (there were several forms), jurisdiction and marriage relationships. As a monk he was able to draft laws for the king, who was overlord as far as the Humber; and to found a school at Canterbury with its scribes. He was a miracle worker in life and after his death. He was buried in his own monastery, which then became known as St Augustine's.

PRAYER AS IN THE MISSAL
Father, you sent St Augustine to be the first apostle to the people of England. May the work he began be renewed in this land and continue

to prosper. Grant this through our Lord Jesus Christ, your Son, who lives and reigns with you and the Holy Spirit, one God, for ever and ever. Amen.

Relevance to our Diocese
Doubtless the large number of catholics coming from Benedictine territory in Warrington suggested St Augustine's name (coupled with that of the English martyrs) for the new parish at Latchford in 1930. Our second parish of St Augustine at Runcorn, was opened in 1969. Their churches came later.

ST BEDE'S ECCLESIASTICAL HISTORY
A blind man of the English race was brought, who having been presented to the priests of the Britons, found no benefit or cure from their ministry. At length Augustine, compelled by real necessity, bowed his knees to the Father of our Lord Jesus Christ, praying that lost sight might be restored to the blind man, and by the corporeal enlightening of one man, the light of spiritual grace might be enkindled in the hearts of many of the faithful. Immediately the blind man received sight, and Augustine was by all declared the preacher of divine truth.

ST COLUMBA, ABBOT (521 - 579)
Feast, June 9th

A blue Iona cross on a white field is the emblem of St Columba.

In 565, "There came to Britain (by curragh) a famous priest and abbot, a monk by habit and life". Columba was born of noble family in Donegal, and had founded monasteries at Derry, Durrow and probably Kells. His motives for coming were possibly penitential as well as missionary, but he set about founding the famous monastery on the island of Iona, which was to become a centre for evangelisation in the northern parts of Scotland, and later in Northumbria, through Lindisfarne.

He converted Brude, king of the Picts, and consecrated Aidan, the Irish king of Dalriada. Not all the many churches and monasteries reputedly founded by him were so, but may have been the work of one of the other fifteen saints of the same name, Colum, meaning dove. He is also known as Columkille, Colum of the churches. He wrote 300 books and poems (he was a bard) and transcribed various scriptures, including a psalter (the Cathach) still to be seen.

Naturally he followed the Celtic tradition of the date of Easter, but was as faithful to Rome as St Patrick had been. He prayed for the pope in his liturgy, which also contained the invocation 'Sancta Maria, ora pro nobis' before the Canon. (It has been suggested that he ignored the Pope and Our Lady). He died at Iona.

PRAYER AS IN THE MISSAL

Lord, warm our hearts with zeal for your kingdom and a longing for its fulfilment: make our lives rich in good works, and so bring us to share in the glory of St Columba, when we see you face to face and are one with you always. Through our Lord Jesus Christ your Son. Amen.

Relevance to our Diocese

St Columba's church, Chester, opened in 1965, was so named by Canon Francis Murphy, himself an Irish priest of truly missionary spirit.

CATHOLIC ENCYCLOPEDIA

He inherited the ardent temperament and strong passions of his race. It has been sometimes said that he was of an angry and vindictive spirit, not only because of his supposed part in the battle of Cooldrevny, but also because of instances related by Adamnan. But the deeds that roused his indignation were wrongs done to others, and the retribution which overtook the perpetrators was rather predicted than actually invoked. Whatever faults were inherant in his nature he overcame, and he stands before the world conspicuous for humility and charity not only towards his brethren, but towards strangers also.

He was generous and warm hearted, tender and kind even to dumb creatures. He was ever ready to sympathize with the joys and sorrows of others. His fasts and vigils were carried to a great extent. The stone pillow on which he slept is said to be still preserved in Iona. His chastity of body and purity of mind are extolled by all his biographers. Notwithstanding his wonderful austerities, Adamnan assures us he was beloved by all, "For a holy joyousness that ever beamed from his countenance revealed the gladness with which the Holy Spirit filled his soul".

ST ALBAN, PROTOMARTYR
(3rd Century)
Feast, June 20th

Alban was martyred in Roman times; and the first to be so commemorated. But it is not known whether he died in the persecution of Diocletian (305) or Decius (254) or Septimus Severus (209). The place is well known, by the town of St Alban's, which was eventually built near the site of Verulamium, where Alban lived.

The gist of Bede's story is that he was a well to do pagan of Roman origin who gave shelter to a priest and was converted by his example. When the persecutors came searching for the priest, Alban exchanged clothes with him and then gave himself up. He refused to sacrifice to the pagan gods and was executed. His appointed executioner refused duty, because of Alban's example and miracles, and was also martyred, "of whom it is apparent, that though he was not regenerated by baptism, yet he was cleansed by the washing of his own blood, and rendered worthy to enter the kingdom of heaven". His actual executioner was punished by blindness. A later story says that the priest was named Amphibalus and he was stoned to death a few days later.

Protomartyr Anglorum, St Alban's emblem consists of a gold saltire on a blue field.

22

PRAYER AS IN NATIONAL CALENDAR

Father, by your grace Saint Alban gave himself up for his friend and was the first in this land to shed his blood for Christ. May we who celebrate his feast be helped continually by his prayers. Grant this through our Lord Jesus Christ your Son, who lives and reigns with you and the Holy Spirit, one God, for ever and ever. Amen.

Relevance to our Diocese

In 1841 St Alban's, Macclesfield, was opened; and in 1859 Dr.Hall acquired a rib of St Alban from Cologne. In 1853 another St Alban's church was opened in Wallasey.

ST PLEGMUND, BISHOP (d.914)
Feast, August 2nd

One of our resident saints, he was a Mercian who lived as a hermit on an island at Plegmundham near Chester (Plemstall on the A57). He helped Alfred to translate Gregory's PASTORAL CARE; and may have had a hand in the ANGLO-SAXON CHRONICLE.

Chosen as Archbishop of Canterbury, he went to Rome, according to custom, to receive the pallium from Pope Formosus. He crowned Edward the Elder in 901, and consecrated the new Minster at Winchester in 908.

By this time the acts and the ordinations of Pope Formosus had (unjustly) been condemned; which may be why Plegmund returned to Rome in 909 to get his own position and his acts confirmed. Another reason would have been to arrange a sub-division of the West Saxon episcopate. As a result , he consecrated seven bishops on the one day — five for Wessex. When he died, in extreme old age, he was buried in his cathedral at Canterbury.

PRAYER

Lord, your holy bishop Plegmund prepared for his pastoral work by years of prayer. Make us realise that we all need to give time to prayer, if we are to achieve anything for your honour and glory. We ask this through Christ our Lord. Amen.

Relevance to our Diocese

St Plegmund's well is still venerated at Plemstall. Four side windows of the sanctuary in St Werburgh's, Chester, relate to him. There is a chapel in his honour at Waverton, near Chester.

ST OSWALD, KING, MARTYR (605 - 642)
Feast, August 3rd

Edwin, his uncle, seized the throne of Northumbria in 616, so Oswald fled to Scotland with his relatives. He became a christian at Iona and returned on Edwin's death in 623. When his brother Eanfrid (kingdom of Deira) and his cousin Osric (kingdom of Bernicia) were both killed, he united those kingdoms under his own rule, as Ethelfrid his father had done. But first he had to defeat the invader, Cadwalla of Wales, which he did at Hevenfelt near Hexham, with a smaller army. Before the battle he set up a large wooden cross, the first in Bernicia, which was still pagan; and asked his troops to pray to God (not to Woden) for victory. This cross was famous, small pieces were used in prayer for miracles of healing.

St Oswald's attributes are the cross of Iona, crown and sceptre, the sword and the martyr's palm.

He sent to Iona for missionaries. St Aidan was the one successful by his kindness. Oswald used to translate for him when he spoke to the people; and the message of Christ was accepted. He gave Aidan the island of Lindisfarne as a monastery and an episcopal see. It became a centre of evangelisation for the north of England. He married Cyneburga, daughter of Cynegils, first christian king of Wessex, to whom he was godfather. He established an overlordship of all the Saxon kingdoms except Mercia and the

East Angles; and had "great power in the north west as far south as Chester and Lancashire".

After only eight years' rule he had to face the invasion of Penda of Mercia (who had killed Edwin). Oswald fell at the battle of Maserfield, praying for those who died with him. His body was dismembered, with the result that relics were sent to many different places. His head was buried at Lindisfarne, and was later transferred to Durham with the body of St Cuthbert.

PRAYER
Father, we thank you for the example of King Oswald, who brought the true faith to his country and bravely died defending both. We thank you through Christ our Lord. Amen.

Relevance to our Diocese
Oswestry (Oswald's cross) claims to be the place of Oswald's death, although this is disputed by Winwick in Lancashire. The large pre-reformation church there is one of seventy in this country. Our presbytery is named Cae Nef, after Oswald's first battle; and our church is called Our Lady Help of Christians and St Oswald. St Oswald's convent is next door, where the Sisters of Charity of St Paul look after the school.

BUTLER'S LIVES
Oswald filled his dominions with churches and monasteries, and whilst he was governing his temporal kingdom, was intent only to labour and pray for an eternal crown. He very often continued in prayer from the time of matins (at midnight), to which he rose with the monks, till daylight; and by reason of his frequent custom of praying or giving thanks to our Lord at all times, he would have his hands on his knees turned upwards to heaven.

ST AIDAN, BISHOP (d.651)
Feast, August 31st

It has been alleged that Aidan was bishop of Clogher, who resigned his see and became a monk at Iona in 630. King Oswald had become a christian at Iona and when he gained his throne, he asked for a missionary to instruct his pagan people of Northumbria. The first missionary was harsh. He failed, blaming the English for being ignorant and unteachable. Aidan heard him reporting back, and said that he ought to have used the milk of mildness instead of the more solid food at first. So they sent Aidan in his place; and he succeeded, with the help of the king, who frequently translated for him.

St Aidan's ability to enlighten through the power of the Gospel is depicted in his emblem. Gold torch with red flames tipped white, blue field.

Oswald gave him the isle of Lindisfarne, cut off from the mainland at every tide, like our own Hilbre island. There he built a monastery, and from there he went on ceaseless visitation of his people, not only to those in Bernicia, who were pagan, but also to those of Deira in the south, who had been evangelised by Paulinus, whose see at York had been vacant for thirty years after his death. From Lindisfarne all the churches in Bernicia had their beginning, from the Tyne to the Tweed; and many in the south, from the Tyne to the Humber. He liberated slave boys, whom he then educated, some for the priesthood. (It was the teaching of Christ that eventually abolished slavery).

He often retired to Farne island for prayer and recollection. As a Columban monk, he observed the Celtic liturgy and Easter customs. (Bede disapproves again). He was very upset by the death of his friend Oswald; but when Oswin, an equally good friend, was murdered in 651, he died a fortnight later of grief, and was buried at Lindisfarne.

PRAYER

Father, your saint Aidan converted the people with the kindness and compassion of Jesus, your Son. Help us to win souls by the same mildness and love. We ask this through Christ our Lord. Amen.

Relevance to our Diocese

The parish of St Aidan, Northern Moor, was split off from St Hilda's, Northenden in 1945. It was Aidan who called Hilda to the monastic life.

ST BEDE

He relates "His love of peace and charity; his continence and humility; his mind superior to anger and avarice, and despising pride and vainglory; his industry in keeping and teaching the heavenly commandments; his diligence in reading and watching; his authority becoming a priest in reproving the haughty and the powerful; and at the same time his tenderness in comforting the afflicted, and relieving or defending the poor. To say all in a few words, as near as I could be informed by those that knew him, he took care to omit none of those things which he found in the apostolical or prophetical writings, but to the utmost of his power endeavoured to perform them all. Those things I much admire in the aforesaid bishop, because I do not doubt that they were pleasing to God; but I do not praise or approve his not observing Easter at the proper time ..."

ST GREGORY, POPE, DOCTOR OF THE CHURCH (c. 540 - 604) APOSTLE OF THE ENGLISH
Feast, September 3rd

Gregory's father Gordianus was a senator who became a deacon; his mother Sylvia became a nun and a saint, like her two sisters. Made Praetor of Rome in 574, Gregory nevertheless entered his own monastery of St Andrew on the Caelian hill; and founded six other monasteries in Sicily. He modified the Benedictine Rule. As a monk, he practised such austerities that they ruined his health for the rest of his life. During this time he was attracted to preach the gospel in pagan England, having met some of the 'angelic Angles' in the slave market.

A red roundel with I H S in gold, representing the Host, and red lions rampant are a reference to St Gregory's Mass. The three bands refer to Gregory's establishing a monastery, the primacy of his office and the introduction of plainchant. All on a gold field.

Ordained one of the seven Roman deacons by the Pope, he was then sent off as Apocrisarius (Nuncio) to Constantinople, seeking help from the Emperor against the Lombards, who were advancing on Rome. (The Goths had captured it twice in his younger days). There he took Eutychus to task for his views on the Resurrection. Returning unsuccessfully to Rome, he saw that he could rely on no help from Constantinople. After five years lecturing and acting as papal secretary, he was elected Pope, to his dismay, in 590; the first monk to become a pope.

In that time of plague and catastrophe, he began the processions, litanies and station Masses in Rome. He looked after refugees, ransomed captives, helped churches looted by the Lombards, three times restored synagogues to Jews who had been evicted from them, and assumed the title Servus Servorum Dei. He wrote a best seller, PASTORAL CARE, later translated by King Alfred, and many other volumes which passed on the work of earlier and greater authors. He reformed the (Gregorian) chant and the liturgy. He was a great administrator of the papal estates, enforced the (existing) laws on celibacy, claimed and exercised supreme authority over western bishops and eastern patriarchs alike. Ignoring the Exarch, he paid off the Lombards and made deals with them. He was the father of the medieval papacy. He converted Arians in Spain and Donatists in Africa; and corrected simony in Gaul.

His peculiar distinction for us is his despatch of St Augustine from his monastery of St Andrew to begin the conversion of the pagans of England. He will always be 'Gregory the Great' for us, as he still is for the rest of the world.

PRAYER AS IN THE MISSAL

Father, you guide your people with kindness and govern us with love. By the prayers of St Gregory give the spirit of wisdom to those you have called to lead your Church. May the growth of your people in holiness be the eternal joy of your shepherds. We ask this through our Lord Jesus Christ your Son, who lives and reigns with you and the Holy Spirit, one God, for ever and ever. Amen.

Relevance to our Diocese

We have a church of St Gregory in Bollington, opened in 1957, to replace the previous church built in 1834.

BUTLER'S LIVES

In the beginning of every month he distributed to all the poor, corn, wine, pulse, cheese, fish, flesh and oil. He appointed officers for every street to send every day necessaries to all the needy sick. Before he ate he always sent off meats from his own table to some poor persons. He was most liberal in redeeming captives taken by the Lombards, for which he permitted the bishop of Fano to break and sell the sacred vessels; and ordered another to do the same.

ST CUTHBERT, BISHOP (c.635 - 687)
Feast, September 4th

Cuthbert, an Anglo-Saxon, was born near Melrose monastery on the banks of the Tweed. It had been founded, like Lindisfarne, by St Aidan. While 'watching his flocks by night', he saw the soul of Aidan being carried up to heaven. It was this that decided him to join the monks at Melrose, for whom he had a great respect. However, it is alleged that he was for some time a soldier, and turned up at the monastery on horseback, carrying a spear. Eata took him along when he went to found the monastery at Ripon, but since the monks would not follow the Celtic customs of Easter, they returned to Melrose, where he became prior. He spent many hours evangelising the lapsed and the heathens between Berwick and Galloway. After the Synod of Whitby, 664, he humbly accepted the Roman customs, and was appointed prior at Lindisfarne, where he had great difficulty in persuading the monks to be equally loyal. Here he often spent whole nights in prayer, and also preached the gospel throughout Northumberland and Durham.

His arms are similar to the arms of Durham. A gold cross, silver lions on a blue field.

Yet he always sought solitude and prayer, so he retired to Farne island in 676, until he was called in 684 to be bishop of Hexham.

He quickly exchanged sees with Eata for Lindisfarne, where he spent the last two years of his life visiting every part of his large diocese.

Even in his lifetime he was called 'wonder worker' and miracles multiplied after his death. For once King Henry VIII's Commissioners respected the body of the saint, although the relics were buried under their original site. His incorrupt body was eventually installed in Durham cathedral and was the pilgrimage centre for the north east of England.

PRAYER

Almighty God, you inspired St Cuthbert with a remarkable spirit of prayer and a deep love of his people. Touch our hearts with the same spirit and love. We ask this through Christ our Lord. Amen.

Relevance to our Diocese

The centre of modern devotion to him is found at St Cuthbert's College, Ushaw near Durham, where the episcopal ring of gold, enclosing a sapphire, taken from his finger in 1537, is preserved: and where, under his patronage, most of the priests from the northern counties are trained. Canon Hugh Welch (junior) was a devoted Ushawman, and gave Cuthbert's name to the church at Mouldsworth, near Chester (for which Mrs Spann did so much).

BUTLER'S LIVES

His very countenance excited those who saw him to a love of virtue. He was so much addicted to compunction and inflamed with heavenly desires, that he could never say Mass without tears. He often moved penitents, who confessed to him their sins, to abundant tears by the torrents of his own, which he shed for them. His zeal in correcting sinners was always sweetened with tender charity and meekness ... As bishop .. he made it everywhere his particular care to exhort, feed and protect the poor . . . his zeal for justice was most ardent, but nothing seemed ever to disturb the peace and serenity of his mind ... under all accidents his countenance was always cheerful, always the same.

ST THOMAS (CANTELUPE)
OF HEREFORD, BISHOP (1218 - 1282)
Feast, October 5th

He seemed destined for a high place in society, being born of a noble Norman family. For his education he went to his uncle (Bishop) Walter Cantelupe, who sent him first to Oxford and then to Paris for philosophy. There he once stole a prop for his window from a neighbour's vineyard, for which he did seven years penance. At Orleans he studied the civil law; and met many eminent people at the first Council of Lyons, including Pope Innocent IV, who made him his chaplain, and also empowered him to hold several benifices at once. By means of sudden visits, he ensured that his vicars fulfilled their duties. Returning to England, he studied canon law at Oxford, where he became a professor and the Chancellor of the University.

He took the barons' side against the king and was their spokesman at Amiens. After the king's defeat at Lewes, he became Chancellor of the kingdom, but retired to Oxford at the death of Simon de Montfort; and he remained on Edward's Privy Council. In 1274 he took part in Lyons II, and the next year was elected bishop of Hereford by the Canons.

Redheaded, rubicund and choleric, he engaged in frequent litigation to resist the encroachment of local nobles on his diocese. More important, he opposed Archbishop Peckham of Canterbury's heavy handed interference with local bishops, again becoming a spokesman - for them - at the Council of Reading. For his persistence, he was excommunicated by the archbishop; and died, still excommunicated, on his way to Rome to appeal to the pope.

In his personal life he was abstemious, prayerful and penitential

The Shrewsbury diocesan coat of arms — a gold sword, green hat and tasselled drapes surrounding a white shield. The shield bears the cross of St Chad in red, with a leopard's head inverted, and a wheatsheaf from the arms of Chester.

31

(wore a hairshirt); and was loved for his care for the poor and for his generosity. 429 miracles after his death he was canonised in 1320 and Hereford became the most important pilgrimage centre in the west of England.

PRAYER
Father, your saint Thomas was an uncompromising champion of the rights of the church and of the people. May we be equally zealous for the rights of others and attentive to our own duties. We ask this through Christ our Lord. Amen.

Relevance to our Diocese
The area of our own diocese, created in 1850, was formerly part of three earlier dioceses - Chester, Lichfield and Hereford. Our diocesan coat of arms incorporates the leopard's head of the diocese of Hereford.

ST WILFRID, BISHOP (634 - 709)
Feast, October 12th

A Northumbrian, Wilfrid was educated at Lindisfarne (which was an escape from a hostile stepmother). Then he went to Lyons, where he refused an offer of marriage to the local bishop's niece; and on to Rome. He returned as a champion of Roman church customs and helped to swing the decision in their favour at the Synod of Whitby in 664.

Phases of his life.
(i) When Wilfrid was abbot at Ripon, where he established Roman usages, to the disgust of the Columban monks, who departed, the king nominated him bishop of York. He went abroad to be consecrated, but was away so long that St Chad took his place; so Wilfrid returned to Ripon, until Theodore restored him to York — Chad bowed out. For some years he energetically looked after his diocese, which extended 'from the Wash to the Forth', building a monastery and a great church at Hexham. He offended the king by

encouraging his wife Etheldreda (Audrey) to become a nun. Theodore took the king's part; and in 678 divided the huge diocese into four, without consulting Wilfrid.

(ii) He left and appealed to Rome - the first appeal made by an Anglo-Saxon. He spent a year preaching in Frisia on the way, thus founding the Anglo-Saxon mission to the people of those parts.

(iii) Rome restored Wilfrid, but the king clapped him into prison, until he went off on another (five year) preaching mission to heathen Sussex and the Isle of Wight, founding a monastery at Selsey. The whole nation became christian.

The shield of St Wilfrid was assigned to him in the 16th Century. He was known as a great 'Fisher of Men' — so the lozenges may suggest a fishing net. Colours — seven voided lozenges, red on a gold field.

(iv) In 686 he returned to Northumbria, but after further disputes with the king over the division of his diocese, he retired to Mercia in 691, where he acted as bishop and founded several more monasteries.

(v) After a Synod of 703 deposed him, he appealed to Rome once more and was again vindicated. He returned to rule the diocese of Hexham (only), but died a few years later, aged 76, in his monastery at Oundle, Northamptonshire.

PRAYER
Father, your bishop Wilfrid strengthened our country's attachment to the see of Peter. May all English christians come to that unity with the Pope and the bishops of the catholic world. We ask this through Christ our Lord. Amen.

Relevance to our Diocese
St Wilfrid's church at Northwich was dedicated to him "after the adjoining church at Davenham which was built by the Cistercians from Vale Royal".

CATHOLIC ENCYCLOPEDIA
Beyond all others of his time, St Wilfrid stands out as the great defender of the rights of the Holy See. For that principle he

fought all his life, first against Colman and the Scottish monks from Iona, and then against Theodore and his successor in the see of Canterbury; and much of his life was spent in exile for this reason. But to him above all others is due the establishment of the authority of the Roman See in England, and for that reason he will always have a very high place among English saints.

BUTLER'S LIVES

How pure his views were, and how remote from avarice and ambition appeared from his charity towards his persecutors, the meekness with which he maintained the rights of his see and the discipline of the church ... If he was rich, he knew of no other use of what he possessed than to employ it in the foundation of churches and in the relief of the poor.

ST EDWARD THE CONFESSOR,
KING (1003 - 1066)
Feast, October 13th

A gold cross and martlets on a blue field. The martlets represented the doves which stood at the top of Edward's sceptre.

Edward had to be brought up in Burgundy by his uncle the Duke, because the Danes, Sweyn and Cnut, occupied the throne of England. But he was the son of Ethelred the Unready, so despite his previous unsuccessful bid for the throne, in which his brother Alfred was killed, he was chosen king in succession to Harthecnut in 1041. For twenty years England enjoyed peace, due to his persistence and skill in restraining Danish and Norman ambition. He started no wars, but drove off a Welsh attack and helped Malcolm III of Scotland against the usurper MacBeth.

34

His one aim was the welfare of his people. He remitted the Danegelt tax and did not require other taxes from them. The 'Laws of good king Edward' were nostalgically remembered in later days. He married Edith, daughter of the powerful Earl Godwin, and lived with her as brother and sister, because of his previous vow of chastity, it is said. (Catholics do not necessarily deny such things. They do happen, by the grace of God).

England owes Westminster Abbey to the pope. When Edward was unable to make the usual Saxon pilgrimage to Rome, which he had promised, the pope commuted his vow into building a church in honour of St Peter. This Edward duly performed, and was buried there, to be followed by many other royals. He was the first to touch people for 'The King's evil' and to cure them (of scrofula). He created bishops who were not of monastic origin; and received papal legates in 1061. His burial in 1066 is depicted in the Bayeux tapestry. He is the only English saint whose body (still incorrupt, there is no doubt about that) was left undisturbed at the Reformation.

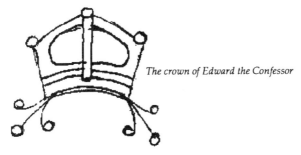

The crown of Edward the Confessor

PRAYER AS IN THE MISSAL
Lord, you raised Saint Edward, king and confessor, to excel in good government and faithful service. May these ideals survive and flourish among us through his prayers. We ask this through Christ our Lord. Amen.

Relevance to our Diocese
Mr and Mrs Edward Lomas built a church in Macclesfield in 1939 and chose Edward as its patron saint. In Runcorn, whose first resident priest was Edward Carter in 1842, we have another St Edward's church and school. In Birkenhead we have Our Lady and St Edward's church, where Bishop Eric Grasar is buried.

MOURRET-THOMPSON'S HISTORY OF
THE CATHOLIC CHURCH

"To preserve peace and promote religion, to enforce the ancient laws, and to diminish the burthen of his people, were the chief objects of his government" (Lingard). The collection of laws published by him still serves as the foundation of the constitution (sic) of the English people. But when the king spoke of going on pilgrimage to Rome in fulfilment of his vow, his advisers, fearing the disorders that might be provoked by his absence, begged him to obtain from the pope a dispensation from it ... The pope gave them for transmission to the king a letter full of fatherly kindness.

"As evidently your presence is necessary in the midst of the English nation, we free you from the vow made by you and from the obligation of performing it. But in return for this dispensation, we command, in the name of holy obedience, that you distribute to the poor the amount of money which you have set aside for your journey to Rome, and that you erect and endow, in honour of the prince of the apostles, in your capital city, a monastery for the glory of God and for the instruction and edification of your people". In carrying out this command, Edward undertook to re-establish the old monastery of St Peter, founded near London at the beginning of christianity in England. It was named Westminster. Such was the origin of the famous Westminster Abbey.

ST PETER OF ALCANTARA,
PRIEST (1499-1562)
Feast, October 19th

Peter was born at Alcantara, near the Spanish border with Portugal, in which countries he spent his life. His father was a lawyer and governor of the town. After studying canon law at Salamanca, Peter joined the Franciscans of Strict Observance at the age of sixteen, when he began his life of amazing austerity and prayer. He guarded his eyes so carefully that he didn't know for a long time that the roof was vaulted and that there grapes were hung up to dry, which he should have distributed. In one convent he knew the other friars only by their voices. When twenty years old, he was sent as Guardian to a new foundation at Bajados. Ordained priest in 1524, "he preferred to preach to the poor, and his sermons breathe the tenderest human sympathy". He was in constant demand as superior and even as Provincial, but he always preferred solitude, and the friars did not like his severe ideas, as expressed at Placentia in 1540.

Eventually he founded his own province of Arabida, stemming from Pedrosa, of the Alcantarines. According to his rule, each cell was to be only 7 feet long (his own was $4^1/2$ feet), the infirmary 13 feet and the church 24 feet. The number of friars was to be not more than eight. They should go barefoot, lie on boards, never, except in illness, eat flesh, fish or eggs, or drink wine. They should spend three hours a day in mental prayer. He wrote a popular book ON MENTAL PRAYER.

The shield is that of the Franciscan Order — a silver cross with the red marks of the stigmata on a brown field. The marks of Our Lord's Passion on hands and feet and side were borne by St Francis, the father of St Peter's Order.

Earlier he had refused to stay and advise King John. In 1555 he declined to become Confessor to the retired Emperor Charles V. He reassured and publicly defended St Teresa of Avila, his fellow mystic, and encouraged her to proceed with her reform of the Carmelites. Kneeling in prayer, he died at the convent of Arenas, while on visitation.

PRAYER

Almighty Father, we cannot match the mystic prayer and the intense austerity of St Peter of Alcantara; but help us to walk with more prayer and penance in the footsteps of your Son Jesus, who is Lord. Amen.

Relevance to our Diocese

Our cathedral in Shrewsbury was built by Bertram, Earl of Shrewsbury, carrying out the wishes of his father John, who had plans drawn up by Augustus Welby Pugin. It was dedicated to our Lady Help of Christians and St Peter of Alcantara. "This was in deference to the founder, who told the bishop that he had received many favours through their intercession".

BUTLER'S LIVES

His prayer and his union with God was habitual. He said Mass with a devotion which astonished others, and often with torrents of tears or with rapture. He was seen to remain in prayer a whole hour, with his arms stretched out and his eyes lifted up without moving. His ecstasies in prayer were frequent and sometimes of long continuance. So great was his devotion to the mystery of the Incarnation and the holy sacrament of the altar that the very mention or thought of them frequently sufficed to throw him in a rapture. In the jubilation of his soul, he sometimes was not able to contain himself from singing the divine praises aloud in a wonderful manner. To do this more freely he sometimes went into the woods, where the peasants who heard him sing took him for one who was beside himself.

ST WINEFRIDE (GWENFREWI), VIRGIN (7th Century) SECONDARY PATRON OF THE DIOCESE Feast, November 3rd

The first life of this seventh century saint was written 500 years after her death. We know more about her cult than about the historical facts. She lived at Holywell (Trefunnen) in Clwyd. Under the influence of her uncle St Beuno, she made a private vow of virginity, intending to become a nun. So she rejected the advances of Caradoc, a Welsh prince from Hawarden. Infuriated by her constant refusal, he struck off her head. Where the head fell a spring appeared, still flowing in the Holy Well.

The story goes that she was restored to life by the prayers of St Beuno, and for many years afterwards she was abbess at Holywell. More likely she moved to Clynnog, then to Henllan and lastly to Gwytherin, because "The Kingdom of Northumbria was pressing upon the borders of North Wales". There she was abbess of a double monastery, St Elwy being the abbot.

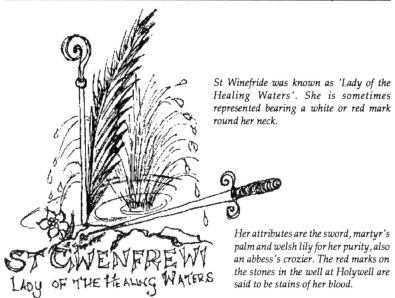

St Winefride was known as 'Lady of the Healing Waters'. She is sometimes represented bearing a white or red mark round her neck.

Her attributes are the sword, martyr's palm and welsh lily for her purity, also an abbess's crozier. The red marks on the stones in the well at Holywell are said to be stains of her blood.

PRAYER

Lord, the vowed virgin St Winefride was willing to be faithful to death; and was faithful in a long life of prayer. We thank you for the many healings you have given us through her intercession at the Holy Well. We thank you through Christ our Lord. Amen.

Relevance to our Diocese

Until 1895, North Wales was part of our diocese. No less than five of our churches are named after her: Monksmoor, Shrewsbury; Brosely; Lymm; Neston and Sandbach. In 1138, her relics were translated to the Benedictine Abbey at Shrewsbury, as described by Ellis Peters. Henry V had walked on pilgrimage from Shrewsbury to Holywell; and probably Edward IV did the same. Lady Margaret Beaumont and her son Henry VII built the still existing chapel, after his victory at Bosworth. Pilgrimages continued in the Penal times; and both Jesuits and secular priests resided in Holywell. In 1629, 14,000 came to celebrate her feast day. Many pilgrims go from our own diocese; and numerous cures have been reported at the Well.

PRAYERS RECITED AT THE WELL
FROM TIME IMMEMORIAL

Almighty and everlasting God, who didst enrich St Winefride with the gift of virginity, grant us we beseech thee by her intercession, to set aside the delights of the world, and to obtain with her the throne of everlasting glory, through Christ our Lord. Amen.

Almighty and everlasting God, grant we humbly beseech thee, that St Winefride may obtain for us such spiritual and temporal benefits as are expedient to thy holy service and our eternal salvation, through Christ our Lord. Amen.

0 blessed Winefride, pure virgin and glorious martyr, so especially chosen, so divinely graced and so wonderfully restored from death to life: hope of all that fly to thee with full confidence and humility; we, though unworthy, yet thy devoted pilgrims, make our petitions unto thee. Sanctuary of piety, look upon us with patient eyes; receive our prayers, accept our offerings; and present our supplications at the throne of mercy, that through thy powerful intercessions, God will be pleased to bless our pilgrimage, and to grant our requests and desires, through Christ our Lord. Amen.

ST EDMUND, BISHOP (1175 - 1240)
Feast, November 16th

Edmund Rich was born in Abingdon. His father entered the monastery at Evesham while his wife was still alive. She attended midnight matins daily, wore haircloth and encouraged Edmund to do the same. Both his sisters became nuns. He found this atmosphere invigorating rather than stifling, and became a rigorous ascetic and a mystic. He studied at Oxford, where he had a vision of the Christ child. Ever after, he signed his forehead each night with the words 'Jesus of Nazareth'. He was sent for further study to Paris, and eventually taught in both universities — logic and theology. Acquiring a reputation as a preacher, he was commissioned by the pope to preach the sixth crusade.

St Edmund was slain by arrows. A gold crown and arrows on a blue field.

In 1222 he became treasurer of Salisbury; and in 1234 the pope appointed him Archbishop of Canterbury (after he had rejected three other candidates). His chosen Chancellor was another saint - Richard of Chichester. He was able to mediate between king and barons, so as to avert a civil war. A doughty reformer, he fell foul of his own monks and clergy. He offended Henry III by demanding him to fill vacant benefices, and not to keep them empty while pocketing the revenues. Edmund also criticised some of his appointments. He made one unsuccessful journey to Rome in 1238, to appeal against his monks and the king; but after little help from a papal delegate, went into exile at Pontigny, where he was buried two years later, after his death at Soissy.

He explained the literal as well as the spiritual sense of the Bible, which he always kissed when he picked it up. His once popular MIRROR OF THE CHURCH is a mystical compendium, a way to spiritual perfection. In 1246, after many miracles, he was canonised only six years after his death; and a year later his body was found incorrupt, as it still remains.

PRAYER
Father, we thank you for St Edmund's holy life and miracles. May they be an encouragement to us to persevere in your way. We ask this through Christ our Lord. Amen.

Relevance to our Diocese

Bishop Edmund Knight founded the Children's Protection and Rescue Society in 1889. St Edmund's Orphanage was built in 1913 and was a constant shelter for 100 children until 1984, when such residential homes were phased out as public policy.

BUTLER'S LIVES
The saint formed many excellent men of prayer, and was himself one of the most experienced doctors of an interior life, and

most enlightened contemplatives in the church. What he chiefly inculcated was a sincere spirit of humility, mortification and holy prayer, and he was principally solicitous to teach christians to pray in affection and spirit. "A hundred thousand persons are deceived in multiplying prayers. I would rather say five prayers devoutly with my heart, than five thousand which my soul does not relish with affection and understanding. 'Sing to the Lord wisely'. What a man repeats by his mouth, that let him feel in his soul".

ST HUGH OF LINCOLN, BISHOP
(c.1140-1200)
Feast, November 17th

Hugh was born at Avalon, Burgundy, lost his mother when he was eight, and was brought up in a convent of Regular Canons, to which his ex-army father eventually retired. He was attracted to the life of prayer and penance of the Carthusians and entered the Grande Chartreuse.

Henry II sent for him to come as Procurator to the Charterhouse which he had founded at Witham, Somerset, (in reparation for the murder of St Thomas Becket). Hugh refused to become Prior until those evicted before the building of the monastery had been re-accommodated and compensated. After seven years at Witham, he reluctantly accepted the bishopric of Lincoln, the largest English diocese. It had been left vacant for sixteen years, so that the pastoral work required was immense. He had a great devotion to the sick, especially lepers. "St Martin's kiss healed the lepers' flesh, but their kiss heals my soul".

Hugh was a happy and lively character, but he couldn't

St Hugh had a pet, a wild swan, which is said to have followed him constantly about his house and grounds. A silver swan on a blue field.

42

stand injustice. He excommunicated the foresters who inflicted death on transgressors of the hunting laws — won their repentance. He defended the Jews against rioting mobs in Lincoln and Northampton. He refused to give benefices to courtiers.

He disarmed the rage of Henry by a personal joke; and placated Richard I in similar fashion; but still refused to pay taxes for the French wars. He revived the famous schools of Lincoln and rebuilt the cathedral, shattered by an earthquake (and joined in the work).

Three times he was papally appointed judge-delegate, because of his wisdom. Shortly before his death he concluded a peace between King John and the French King Philip Augustus. He was canonised only 20 years later. His pet swan is his emblem — or a chalice with the Infant Jesus superimposed.

PRAYER

Lord, your holy bishop Hugh of Lincoln defended the rights of the poor and oppressed, and opposed the injustice of kings. Help us to imitate his care for the sick, his devotion to duty and his love of prayer, through Christ our Lord. Amen.

Relevance to our Diocese

The parish priest responsible for initiating the new parish of St Hugh, West Timperley, was Canon Hugh Welch (senior); and the bishop of the day was Hugh Singleton. Their devotion to such a "beautiful sacerdotal figure" (Ruskin thus described him) was both understandable and acceptable. For many years St Hugh's Senior School for boys was one of the foremost schools in Birkenhead.

BUTLER'S LIVES

He distinctly foretold his death; spent almost his whole time in fervent addresses to God, or in devout colloquies with his angel-guardian or the saints. He received the Viaticum and Extreme Unction on St Matthew's day, but survived until 17th November. On that day he caused many monks and priests, besides his chaplains, to recite the divine office in his chamber. Seeing them weep, he said many tender things to comfort them, and laying his hands upon them one by one, recommended them to the divine custody. His voice beginning to fail, he ordered the floor to be swept and a cross of blessed ashes to be strewn upon it, and whilst the 90th psalm at Compline was said, would be lifted out of bed and laid upon that cross, in which posture, as he was repeating the Nunc Dimittis, he calmly expired.

ST HILDA, VIRGIN (614-680)
Feast, November 17th

Converted by Paulinus in 627, at the age of thirteen, and baptised with her uncle Edwin of Northumbria, she spent her first thirty three years in secular life. At the request of St Aidan, she built a small monastery on the banks of the Wear, then moved to Hartlepool as abbess (South Shields is a corruption of St Hilda).

In 657 she re-founded a double monastery at Whitby, where she acquired libraries, insisted on the study of scripture, and instructed future clerics in Latin and literature. Five bishops were

trained by her, including St John of Beverley and St Wilfrid of York. She hosted the Synod of Whitby in 664, when she humbly accepted the Roman date of Easter, although she had supported the Celtic party. She sided with Theodore when he deprived her ex-pupil Wilfrid of his episcopal see. For seven years before her death she suffered from a grievous fever, but this did not prevent her life of prayer and action.

The coiled serpents refer to the legend of St Hilda's prayers changing dangerous snakes into stones. Gold serpents on a blue field.

PRAYER

Lord, you endowed St Hilda with the gifts of prayer and good counsel, with a love of learning and the sacred scripture. Give us holy women and men with these same gifts, to guide us on our way through life. We ask this through Christ our Lord. Amen.

Relevance to our Diocese

St Hilda is venerated in our church at Northenden. Her name was given to the original church by Mrs Zeba Ward, before it was acquired by Bishop Allen in 1904. For some years there was a St Hilda's school in Wallasey.

ST BEDE

She put this monastery (Whitby) under the same regular discipline as she had done the former; and taught there the strict observance of justice, piety, chastity and other virtues and particularly of peace and charity; so that, after the example of the primitive church, no person was there rich, and none poor, all being in common to all, and none having any property. Her prudence was so great, that not only indifferent persons, but even kings and princes as occasion offered, asked and received her advice. She obliged those who were under her direction to attend so much to the reading of the Holy Scriptures, and to exercise themselves so much in works of justice, that many might be found there fit for ecclesiastical duties, and to serve at the altar ...

Thus this servant of Christ, Abbess Hilda, whom all that knew her called Mother, for her singular piety and grace, was not only an example of good life to those that lived in her monastery, but afforded occasion of amendment and salvation to many who lived at a distance ...

ST THOMAS BECKET, BISHOP, MARTYR (1118 - 1170) PATRON OF THE PASTORAL CLERGY OF ENGLAND
Feast, December 29th

Born in Cheapside of Norman parents, he studied at Paris University. At first an accountant, he became a clerk in the household of Theobald, Archbishop of Canterbury, and read law at

These birds, the Cornish Choughs, are said to have been known in mediaeval days at St Thomas' birds. Black choughs with red legs and beaks on a silver field.

Bologna and Auxerre. As Archdeacon of Canterbury, he caught the eye of Henry II, who made him Chancellor in 1155. For seven years he was statesman, diplomat and soldier, a hunting and hawking enthusiast, with an ostentatious lifestyle. He pleased the king, but not always the church.

Appointed Archbishop of Canterbury, he underwent a spiritual conversion, wore a hairshirt (secretly), and adopted the simple manners of his predecessor. He first annoyed the king by resigning his Chancellorship. Then disagreements arose over the rights of the church to excommunicate royal tenants and to try clerics in church courts. Henry's view of such rights were embodied in the Constitutions of Clarendon. Refusing to accept them, Thomas fled to France and appealed to the pope (a right denied by the king). During those seven years abroad, the king persecuted his family and expropriated his lands. Thomas published the papal excommunications of those who had crowned Henry's son in defiance of the pope.

In 1170 Thomas and Henry patched up a reconciliation, whereupon Thomas returned to a great welcome at Canterbury. But his enemies stirred up the anger of the king, who bitterly wondered why nobody would rid him of this turbulent priest. Four knights acted upon this outrageous suggestion (which he had not seriously intended). After a furious verbal attack, they murdered Thomas in his own cathedral.

All Europe was aghast. Henry did private and public penance. Miracles began to happen, twenty in the first year. Thomas was canonised and Henry reconciled to the pope within three years. Canterbury became a major centre of pilgrimage for those who came "the blissful, holy martyr for to seek".

PRAYER AS IN THE DIVINE OFFICE

Almighty God, you enabled St Thomas Becket to lay down his life with undaunted spirit for the rights of your church. Let his prayer help us to deny ourselves for Christ in this life, and so to find our true life in heaven. We make our prayer through our Lord Jesus Christ, your Son. Amen.

Relevance to our Diocese

We have a church of St Thomas Becket at Tarporley, near Chester, and for some years there was a St Thomas Becket school in Moreton.

From ST THOMAS OF CANTERBURY, Margaret Harvey, CTS.

Those still near to Becket heard him commit his cause to God, Our Lady, St Denis and St Alphege. At that moment FitzUrse sliced off the top of his scalp; and severely wounded Edward Grim, who was standing with his arms round the Archbishop, trying to shield him. Becket stood there, blood streaming down his face, praying "Into thy hands 0 Lord, I commend my spirit". He was struck several times more. Finally he fell to the ground with the whole top of his skull severed and the blood pouring out over the pavement. Mauclerc shouted out "Let us away, knights, this fellow will rise up no more".

* * *

Our Saints in Their Times

200	St Alban d c 209	Roman Conquest from 43 AD 61 Boudica's rebellion 122 Hadrian's Wall
300	St George 3rd/4th C	367 Invasion of Picts and Scots.
400	St Patrick to Ireland 432	408 Roman troops leave. Angles, Saxons, Jutes settle in East
500	Columba 521-597 Gregory 540-604 Augustine d 605	516 Arthur defeats invaders. Britons survive. 577 Ceawlin of Wessex separates Britons of Wales and Cornwall
600	Winefride 7th C Oswald d 602 Aidan d 651 Chad d 672 Hilda d 680 Cuthbert d 678 Werburgh d 700 Wilfrid d 709	664 Synod of Whitby 672 Hertford Heptarchy gradually established — Northumbria, Mercia, East Anglia, Essex, Kent, Sussex and Wessex
700	Milburga d 700 Bede 673-735 Walburga d 779 Alcmund d 800	Rule of eight Bretwaldas 797 Death of Offa — his Dyke at Chester and Oswestry
800		875 Danish army over-runs East 871-899 Reign of Alfred
900	Plegmund d 914	899-939 Danelaw reconquered
1000	Edward c 1004-1066	1016-1035 Cnut reigns 1066 Norman Conquest 1086 Domesday Book

Our Saints in Their Times

1100	1078-1134 Stephen Harding 1118-1170 Thomas Becket	1139-1154 Civil War in Stephen's reign
1200	1170-1246 Edmund of Abingdon 1218-1282 Thomas of Hereford	1215 Magna carta 1264 Barons' War 1277 Edward I annexes Wales
1300		1296-1336 Scottish wars 1348 Black Death 1341 Peasants' Revolt 1399 Henry IV
1400		1455-1487 Wars of the Roses
1500	1499-1562 Peter of Alcantara	1529-1539 Henry VIII's Reforming Parliament. Dissolution of monasteries. 1588 Armada

A Calendar of These Saints

FEBRUARY	3	Werburgh
	25	Walburga
MARCH	2	Chad
	17	Patrick
	19	Alcmund
APRIL	17	Stephen Harding
	23	George
MAY	19	Milburga
	21	Dedication of the Cathedral
	24	Our Lady Help of Christians
	25	Bede
	27	Augustine
	28	Robert Johnson **
		John Sherd **
JUNE	9	Columba
	20	Alban
JULY	19	John Plessington **
AUGUST	2	Plegmund
	3	Oswald
	28	Thomas Holford **
	30	Margaret Ward **
		Richard Martin **
	31	Aidan
SEPTEMBER	3	Gregory
	4	Cuthbert
	15	Our Lady of Pity
OCTOBER	1	Ralph Crocket **
		Edmund Campion **
		Robert Wilcox**
	5	Thomas of Hereford
	12	Wilfrid
	13	Edward
	19	Peter of Alcantara
NOVEMBER	3	Winefride
	16	Edmund
	17	Hugh of Lincoln
		Hilda
DECEMBER	29	Thomas Becket

* *Also included are the feasts of the martyrs written about in*
'Nine Martyrs of Shrewsbury Diocese' by the same author

50

SOURCES

ECCLESIASTICAL HISTORY OF ENGLAND; *St Bede*
HISTORY OF THE CATHOLIC CHURCH; *Mourret-Thompson*
LIVES OF THE SAINTS; *Alban Butler*
OXFORD DICTIONARY OF SAINTS; *David Hugh-Farmer*
PAMPHLETS —
  St Thomas of Canterbury; *Rev W.J. Anderson*
  St Wilfrid; *Henry Mayr-Harding*
  St Edmund of Abingdon; *Rev John Crozier*
  St Patrick; *Donald A. Kerr*
PENGUIN DICTIONARY OF SAINTS; *Donald Attwater*
THE DIVINE OFFICE
THE ROMAN MISSAL

MISS BERNADETTE BOWES for her illustrations, in addition to the
above, used the following books:-

BEASTS AND SAINTS; *Helen Waddell*
BURTON IN WIRRAL, A HISTORY; *ed. Paul Booth*
DICTIONARY OF CHRISTIAN LORE AND LEGEND; *J.C.J. Metford*
FIELD GUIDE TO BRITISH BIRDS; *Reader's Digest*
HERALDRY, SOURCES, SYMBOLS AND MEANING; *O. Neubecker*
MEDIAEVAL SHERBOURNE; *Joseph Fowler*
MUIR'S HISTORICAL ATLAS; *Ancient, Mediaeval and Modern*
OLD CHESHIRE CHURCHES; *Raymond Richards*
OLD ENGLAND, A PICTORIAL MUSEUM; *ed. Charles Knight*
SAINTS AND THEIR EMBLEMS IN ENGLISH CHURCHES; *R. Milburn*
SAINTS, SIGNS AND SYMBOLS; *W. Ellwood Post*